President Clinton's

AMAZING ARKANSAS

500 Fabulous Facts

Compiled by Ken Beck and Terry Beck
Premium Press America/Spring Creek Books
Nashville, Tennessee

AMAZING ARKANSAS
Published by
Premium Press America/Spring Creek Books
Nashville, Tennessee

Copyright © 1993 by Ken Beck and Terry Beck

All rights reserved. No part of this book may be reproduced or transmitted in any form or by any means, electronic or mechanical, including photocopying, recording, or by any information storage and retrieval system, without the written permission of the Publisher, except where permitted by law.

ISBN: 0-9637733-3-X

Library of Congress Catalog Card Number
93-86541

Premium Press America books are available at special discounts for bulk purchases for sales promotions, premiums, fund-raising, or educational use. For information contact Premium Press America, P.O. Box 159015, Nashville, TN 37215; Phone (615) 352-3922.

Cover design by L. Mayhew Gore Art
Layout by Brent Baldwin

Printed in Nashville, Tennessee, by Douglas Printing.

October 1993

2 3 4 5 6 7 8 9 10

AMAZING ARKANSAS

DEDICATION

To Daddy — Alton A. Beck — the best man from Ben Lomond, Arkansas, we've ever known; the best man from Arkansas we've ever known; the best man we've ever known.

ACKNOWLEDGEMENTS

Hearty Arkansas thank y'alls go to such fine folks as Bob Lancaster, Tyler Hardeman, Kit Bakker, Brenda McClain, Brent Baldwin, Jim Clark, Marc Muncy, Ray Muncy, Glenda Washam, and many others we talked to across the state of Arkansas, who helped us turn nuggets of information into amazing facts.

INTRODUCTION

Since the election of William Jefferson Clinton to the presidency of the United States in November 1992, more and more Americans have been discovering one of the best-kept secrets of the twentieth century — Arkansas is an amazing place.

Of course, Arkansans have known this all along, even before the territory became a state back in 1836.

Those of us who have grown up here or who have lived here for any length of time are witnesses to Arkansas' two major assets: its incredible array of natural resources, which have filled the state with dazzling beauty and awesome geographical wonders, and its people. Arkansans are friendly, hard-working and easy-going folks.

In fact, when one Arkansan bumps into a fellow Arkansan in another state or far off place, even if they've never met before, it's like old home week. And while

Arkansans are loyal to one another and their Razorbacks, they're also accommodating to newcomers and visitors. Few states offer more smiles per the miles.

With *Amazing Arkansas* we've tried to mention a few of the state's most famous natives, point out some of its best physical features and tourist attractions, display some basic nuts-and-bolts facts and also look at some of the more unusual occurrences and humorous events in its history.

Once you take a peek at some of the facts in here, we believe you'll agree, even more than you'd ever imagined, that Arkansas is an amazing state.

Ken Beck and Terry Beck,
North Little Rock, Arkansas, October, 1993.
Sylvan Hills High School, classes of 1970 and 1976.
Harding College, classes of 1974 and 1980.

AMAZING ARKANSAS

1. The Arkansas Razorback cheer goes like this:

   "Woo, Pig, Sooie!
   Woo, Pig, Sooie!
   Woo, Pig, Sooie! Razorbacks!"

2. It has been said that Arkansas, with its great variety of natural resources, is the only state that could have a wall built around it, isolating it from the rest of the world, and still survive and prosper.

3. The house shown at the beginning of the TV show *Designing Women,* the Villa Marre, is located at the corner of East Fourteenth and Scott streets in Little Rock and was built in 1881.

4. Legend has it that Ink, Arkansas, was named by postal officials who filled in a form which asked for the town's new name. The instructions said "Write in ink" and they did.

AMAZING ARKANSAS

5. President William Jefferson (Bill) Clinton was born William Jefferson Blythe IV at the Julia Chester Hospital in Hope, Arkansas, on August 19, 1946.

6. Arkansas is one of the top five states as a place to relocate for retirement.

7. In White County, the Black Creek runs into the Little Red River, which runs into the White River, but the Black Creek is not black, the Little Red is not red and the White River is not white; also, Red Lake is not red, Blue Lake is not blue, Clear Lake is not clear and Big Lake is not big, and Horseshoe Lake is not shaped like a horseshoe.

8. Iced ducks fell out of the sky in November 1973 during a hailstorm over Stuttgart. Make that a quacker on the rocks.

9. Hector, Arkansas, was named for President Grover Cleveland's bulldog.

AMAZING ARKANSAS

10. Dillard's, one of the nation's most successful department store chains with 223 stores, has its headquarters in Little Rock. Its founder, William Dillard, opened his first store in 1938 in Nashville, Arkansas. On his worst day in business, Dillard took in $1.62 at his Nashville store. Today, his stores bring in about seven million dollars per day.

11. Bill Clinton's favorite film is *High Noon,* which he has viewed at least 19 times. He's also a big fan of *Casablanca.* Play it again, Bill.

12. Born in Bentonville, Arkansas, on November 12, 1905, Louise Thaden set the first altitude record for women pilots in 1929, and in 1936 in the Bendix Trophy Race, she set the record time between Los Angeles and New York City of 14 hours and 55 minutes.

13. Bill Clinton is addicted to crossword puzzles and works them in ink.

AMAZING ARKANSAS

14. NASA stored moon rocks in Hot Springs' hot spring water, while searching for signs of life, because of the liquid's natural sterility.

15. Tyson Foods ("Feeding you like family"), which makes its headquarters in Springdale, is the largest poultry company in the country, processing 25 million chickens a week. And that's no yolk.

16. The first Wal-Mart store was established in Rogers, Arkansas, in 1962. Today, the headquarters of the world's largest retailer, with more than 2,000 stores in 43 states and 371,000 employees, is located in Bentonville, Arkansas.

17. Boots, a Heber Springs cat, has a "fishing license" from the Arkansas Game and Fish Commission. The four-pound, female feline pounces from the bank into the Little Red River to catch trout, one of which was 12 inches long. In her spare time, Boots also catches moles, although she has no hunting license.

AMAZING ARKANSAS

18. Jerry Jones, owner of the 1993 Super Bowl champion Dallas Cowboys, grew up in North Little Rock, Arkansas, and played college football on the undefeated 1964 national championship Arkansas Razorback team with Jimmy Johnson, head coach of the Cowboys. Jones and Johnson were college roommates.

19. The world's largest soda float was concocted Oct. 14, 1990, at the Arkansas State Fairgrounds with 1,200 pounds of Coleman Quality Chekd Dairy's skim milk and 936 gallons of Coca-Cola. Two straws please.

20. In 1832, the Hot Springs area became the first public land in the United States to be set aside for protection by the federal government, making it unofficially the first national park.

21. Alan Ladd, star of the classic western *Shane,* was born in Hot Springs on September 13, 1913. "Come back, Shane."

AMAZING ARKANSAS

22. Little Rock became a Little Detroit in 1919 when the Climber Motor Corporation began manufacturing four-cylinder, 40-horsepower, touring cars. About 200 of the cars were sold before the company went out of business in 1924. Only two are known to exist today and one of them is in the Museum of Automobiles on Petit Jean Mountain. Climber also made 100 pick-up trucks.

23. Chicago Bulls basketball star Scottie Pippen was born in Hamburg on Sept. 25, 1965. He began playing ball in the 10th grade and was a team manager his freshman year in college. Three years later he was the fifth pick in the 1987 NBA first-round draft.

24. Bill Clinton was the 42nd governor of Arkansas and the 42nd U.S. President.

25. Lake City has what may be the only drawbridge in the world that has never been raised. It was christened with a bottle of beer in 1934.

AMAZING ARKANSAS

26. Systematics, based in Little Rock, is the nation's leading provider of data processing services and software to the financial industry.

27. When Bill Clinton was first elected governor of Arkansas his salary was $35,000 a year. In 1992, he received a raise to $60,000. In 1993, his salary was raised to $200,000 when he was promoted by the American people to the White House.

28. During the Depression, the Pacific Coast Whaling Company brought an embalmed whale through Arkansas on a railroad flatcar and charged ten cents admission to see it. The whale, named Colossus, was an outstanding success. For another dime, spectators could buy a miniature copy of the book of Jonah. A whale of a deal, I'd say.

29. Burns Park in North Little Rock, with its 1,575 acres, is the second largest municipal park in the United States.

AMAZING ARKANSAS

30. Arkansas' Maurice Lee "Footsie" Britt Jr., who played pro football for the Detroit Lions, was the first soldier to win the nation's three highest honors: the Congressional Medal of Honor, the Distinguished Service Cross and the Silver Star. He is a cousin to Dorothy Lamour.

31. Baseball Hall of Famer Brooks Robinson was born in Little Rock on May 18, 1937. The Baltimore Oriole was a Golden Glove whiz at third base and as a Little Rock high school student won a locker full of prizes for his classmates at a pitching booth one year at the Arkansas State Fair.

32. The Booneville library contains a miniature flag that was carried to the moon by Apollo 10.

33. That darn Clinton family cat, Socks, is the 12th official cat in residence at the White House. He got his name because his white feet resemble socks. He has a sister, Midnight, who still lives in Little Rock.

AMAZING ARKANSAS

34. The longest pontoon bridge in the world was built on the Arkansas River near Russellville in 1889-91 and was not replaced until 1929. Teddy Roosevelt walked across it in 1912. Bully for him.

35. Gilbert Anderson, who was born in Little Rock on March 21, 1882, went to Hollywood and became Bronco Billy Anderson, the silver screen's first cowboy hero. He starred in 1903's *The Great Train Robbery* and made over 400 Bronco Billy westerns.

36. Alma lays claim to the title of "Spinach Capital of the World" since 56 percent of the world's spinach is canned there. An eight-foot statue of Popeye and the world's largest spinach can are on display there. Well, blow me down.

37. The "hum-burger" at Paragould's Hamburger Station is rated one of the best hamburgers in the nation by USA Today. It costs $1.35 and the ingredients include beef, grilled onions, mustard and pickles.

AMAZING ARKANSAS

38. Bill and Hillary Clinton honeymooned in Acapulco. Her parents and two brothers, Hugh and Tony, also came along.

39. The Arkansas River is the third longest in the U.S. and the 36th longest in the world. With its head near Leadville, Colorado, the Arkansas River's 1,459 mile-length makes it the longest river flowing into the Mississippi-Missouri River system.

40. When opening ceremonies were held on September 12, 1965, Little Rock's KATV 2,000-foot television tower was the world's second tallest structure, 528 feet taller than the Empire State Building. Present for the occasion were ABC television stars Linda Evans of *The Big Valley,* Larry Storch of *F Troop* and Ted Cassidy, Lurch of *The Addams Family.* You rang?

41. Howard "Rip" Collins of Heber Springs caught a world record 40-pound, 4-ounce trout on May 9, 1992, in the Little Red River.

AMAZING ARKANSAS

42. Among some of Bill Clinton's favorite games are Pictionary, Hearts, Trivial Pursuit and pinochle. He and Hillary especially enjoy competing with their close friends, television producers Harry Thomason and Linda Bloodworth-Thomason.

43. One of the world's largest collections of Bibles is in the Bible Museum in Eureka Springs. It contains 7,000 rare Bibles and religious manuscripts written in 625 different languages. That's a lot of Good Books.

44. In 1927, the new Little Rock Senior High School was labeled "America's most beautiful high school" by the National Association of Architects and was the largest high school in the nation until the 1940s.

45. Among Bill Clinton's favorite snacks are Coca-Cola on the rocks, doughnuts, barbecue, chicken enchiladas, lemon chess pie, peanut butter sandwiches, chips and dip and mango chutney ice cream. No wonder he jogs nearly every day.

AMAZING ARKANSAS

46. The White River Monster was spotted June 19, 1971, near Newport and described as a smooth, gray and very long creature the size of a boxcar. A representative of the International Bureau of UFOs thought the creature might be a type-3 alien, an experimental alien sent to Earth as a test. However a CBS film crew could not substantiate the theory.

47. Arkansas is the Number 1 rice-producing state in America, and Riceland Foods of Stuttgart is the world's largest processor of rice.

48. Winslow, Arkansas, was the first town in America to elect a woman mayor, Maude Duncan. She became mayor in 1925 and was also the town's pharmacist and newspaper editor.

49. Maybelline Incorporated of North Little Rock is the world's leader of mass-produced domestic cosmetics.

50. The Arkansas State Tree is the loblolly pine.

AMAZING ARKANSAS

51. The Maynard City Jail is probably the state's smallest jail at 60 square feet. It has a dirt floor, and the metal door was constructed from two wagon wheels. The first occupant of the calaboose was a man who helped construct it. Photos are allowed when the jail is not in use. Bea, the city clerk, has the key in her desk.

52. Stuttgart, Arkansas, hosts the World Championship Duck Calling Contest. "Here, Daffy, here boy."

53. After George D. Hay visited a hoedown in Mammoth Spring as a reporter for the *Memphis Commercial Appeal* in the 1920s, he was inspired to start Nashville's Grand Ole Opry. The town celebrates every Labor Day weekend with "Solemn Old Judge Days."

54. The first white man to enter Arkansas was Spanish explorer Hernando de Soto in 1541, which was 79 years before the Pilgrims landed on Plymouth Rock.

AMAZING ARKANSAS

55. The EPA named Lake Ouachita the second-cleanest lake in the United States. Lake Conway is the largest Game and Fish Commission lake in the United States. Lake Chicot is the largest natural lake in the state.

56. University of Arkansas basketball star Sidney Moncrief was born in Little Rock on September 21, 1957. He played pro ball with the Milwaukee Bucks and now owns the Sydney Moncrief Pontiac-Buick-GMC Truck dealership in Sherwood.

57. On the Belle Point Ranch in Lavaca, Arkansas, is what could be the world's largest Budweiser beer can— an advertisement has been painted on a silo which could hold enough brew to fill 121,318 six-packs or 727,908 bottles of beer on the wall.

58. Author Ernest Hemingway lived off and on from 1927-1940 in Piggott, Arkansas, after he married native Pauline Pfieffer. He often trapped and duck-hunted in Stuttgart.

AMAZING ARKANSAS

59. Although Bill Clinton is left-handed, he golfs right-handed. His score generally runs from 85 to 100. Fore!

60. In 1881, the Arkansas general assembly decided to pronounce the state name Ark-an-saw instead of Ar-Kansas.

61. A White River pearl is nestled in the Royal Crown of England.

62. Academy Award-winning actress Mary Steenburgen (for *Melvin and Howard*) grew up in North Little Rock and was executive producer of the 1987 film *The End of the Line*, which was shot in Arkansas and featured a number of native Arkansas actors, including Levon Helm and Tess Harper.

63. Judge Isaac Parker, "the hanging judge," hanged 79 outlaws between the years 1875-1896 in Fort Smith, Arkansas.

AMAZING ARKANSAS

64. Arkansas' state musical instrument is the fiddle.

65. Bill Clinton graduated from Hot Springs High School where, as a member of the Trojan band, he earned All-State Band honors on the saxophone. In high school he was also a member of the Beta Club, the National Honor Society, the chorus and the Key Club.

66. The Rollin' Razorbacks, based in Sherwood, won their second consecutive National Wheelchair Basketball Championship title in 1991. Four team members won gold medals at the 1992 Paralympic Games in Barcelona, Spain.

67. In 1945, the United States Department of Agriculture's Miscellaneous No. 454 stated that "Arkansas women are on the average the shapeliest in the nation." That figures.

68. The first school in Arkansas was Dwight Mission, built in 1820 near Russellville for Cherokee children.

AMAZING ARKANSAS

69. Hot Springs Mountain Valley Water is the second largest bottler of mineral water in the world. Among those who have loved to chug the beverage have been John Lennon, Elvis Presley, Frank Sinatra, Calvin Coolidge, Joe Louis, Anwar Sadat, Muhammad Ali, and Secretariat.

70. Among the many and varied names of Arkansas towns and communities are Bald Knob, Calico Rock, Arkadelphia, Amity, Oil Trough, Hogeye, Cotton Plant, Umpire, Fifty Six, Forty Four, Figure Five, Welcome Home, Weiner, Lost Corner, Three Brothers, Number Nine, Blue Ball, Light, Pencil Bluff, Marble, Judsonia, Snowball, Tomato, Greasy Corner, Damascus, Jerusalem, Palestine, Paris, Holland, England and Egypt. The most popular place name in the state, with 12 different locales, is Oak Grove.

71. Winthrop Rockefeller, grandson of John D. Rockefeller, was governor of Arkansas from 1967-1971.

AMAZING ARKANSAS

72. Al Capp's *Li'l Abner* cartoon strip was set in the fictional community of Dogpatch. Today there is a Dogpatch USA amusement park near Harrison, Arkansas.

73. Long-driving professional golfer John Daly grew up in Dardanelle and played for the University of Arkansas golf team before winning his PGA title at the age of 25 in 1991. He drove a long way to win the tournament. His Wilson golf balls feature a red razorback hog and the word "kill" (Daly's motto) stamped on them.

74. One of Bill Clinton's favorite foods is a hot cheeseburger. That's a burger with jalapeno cheese, lettuce and tomato.

75. Hillary Clinton, a 1973 Yale law graduate, has twice been voted as one of the top 100 lawyers in the country. She was born Hillary Diane Rodham in Chicago, Illinois, on October 26, 1947.

AMAZING ARKANSAS

76. Elvis Presley got his first G.I. haircut on March 25, 1958, at Fort Chaffee, Arkansas. He was clipped by James B. Peterson for sixty-five cents. Wonder if it chafed him?

77. Bill Clinton went to grammar school at Brookwood Elementary, St. John's Catholic School and Ramble Elementary, all in Hot Springs.

78. Old Fort Days' Futurity and Rodeo in Fort Smith hosts the world's richest barrel race, which is held annually near the end of May. First place prize money in 1992 was over $60,000 and the entry fee is $600 per rider.

79. When the Victory Service League sponsored a national campaign during World War II, Newport schoolteacher Martha Newsome set the national record by collecting 2,600 ladies' hose. She accomplished the feat by talking her fourth-grade class into canvassing practically every house in town.

AMAZING ARKANSAS

80. The four blue stars on the Arkansas flag represent the Confederacy and the other three countries which she has been a part of — France, Spain and the United States. And the diamond stands for the state's famous diamond mine.

81. Sultane Magnolia Belle, born in 1926 in Columbia County, Arkansas, was the world-champion Jersey milk cow at producing butterfat. In 1936, she was milked every eight hours by Melbourn Walthall for 365 days, and produced 1,043 pounds of butterfat. Belle was owned by Magnolia A&M College. Udderly amazing.

82. Residents of Arkansas are called Arkansans, but they have also been called Arkansians, Arkansawyers and Arkies.

83. There are 47 hot springs at Hot Springs National Park where the 4,000-year-old thermal waters flow at about 143 degrees.

AMAZING ARKANSAS

84. The highest point in Arkansas is Mount Magazine, 2,753 feet above sea level, in Logan County. It is also the only locale between the Alleghenies and the Rockies where the fern *woodsia scapulina* can be found.

85. The Ozark Scottish Festival is held the last weekend in April each year in Batesville.

86. Roger Clinton, brother to the President, is a professional singer on the Atlantic Records label. He used to perform audience warm-ups for the TV show *Designing Women*.

87. Mountain View hosts an annual Bean Fest with free pinto beans, cornbread and onions. Its tall-tale-telling contest is called "The Big Blowout."

88. The Arkansas state capitol is built on the site of a former penitentiary and for this reason it is not "squared" with the other streets in the area.

AMAZING ARKANSAS

89. The Hinderliter Grog Shop, which was built in the 1820s, is the oldest house in Little Rock.

90. Arkansas teen David O. Dodd, "the boy martyr of the Confederacy," was hanged in Little Rock on January 8, 1864, by the Union Army because they suspected that he was a Confederate spy.

91. In 1982, Arkansas provided both Miss America, Elizabeth Ward of Russellville, and Miss USA, Terri Utley of Cabot. In 1964, Miss Arkansas, Donna Axum, was selected as Miss America.

92. Baptists make up the state's largest single religious group.

93. The Lindbergh Monument in Lake Village commemorates the first night flight made by Charles Lindbergh, which occurred in 1923 after the famed aviator made an emergency landing in a resident's yard.

AMAZING ARKANSAS

94. Billed as "The Game of the Century," the contest between Texas and Arkansas, the No. 1 and No. 2 college football teams in the nation at the time, was played before President Richard M. Nixon and a senator from Texas, George Bush, in 1969. We're not telling who won.

95. Rogers, Arkansas, is the home of the Daisy Manufacturing Company, maker of fine BB-guns, including the Red Ryder BB- gun. The Daisy International Air Gun Museum in Rogers has the world's most complete collection of air guns, including the original Red Ryder BB-gun.

96. Bill Clinton's high school nickname was Billy "Vote" Clinton because he campaigned so often.

97. The highest temperature ever recorded in Arkansas was 120 degrees on August 10, 1936, at Ozark. The lowest temperature ever recorded in the state was minus 29 degrees on February 13, 1905, at Pond.

AMAZING ARKANSAS

98. Howard County was home of the largest peach orchard in the world in 1938. The orchard had over one million trees, enough to supply a peach for every person in the United States. Peachy keen, huh?

99. In 1978, Bill Clinton was the nation's youngest governor at the age of 32. Yet none dared call him Billy the Kid. Just kidding, Bill.

100. Gospel/pop singer Al Green was born in Forrest City on April 13, 1946. He has recorded four gold albums.

101. Berryville is the "turkey capital of Arkansas" and produces a half a million turkeys annually, while Yellville hosts the National Wild Turkey Calling Contest and Turkey Trot Festival. Who gobbles?

102. In 1957, Frank Headlee, a former mayor of Searcy, invented a miniature, musical commode which he called the "Tinkle Pot." They were a No. 1 hit across the nation as they sold for about $9 each.

AMAZING ARKANSAS

103. During the Civil War, 15,000 Arkansans fought for the North, while 60,000 Arkansans fought for the South. The largest Civil War battle west of the Mississippi was in Arkansas at the Battle of Pea Ridge in 1862.

104. POM (Park-O-Meter) of Russellville manufactured the world's first parking meters in 1935. Deposit dime here for 30 minutes parking.

105. Arkansas' Fouke Monster was first spotted in the 1940s but on May 25, 1971, Bobby Ford sighted what he described as a giant, stooped monkey with big red eyes that stank and had a piercing scream. In 1973, the Texarkana Jaycees offered a $10,000 reward for its capture. The monster was the subject of the film *The Legend of Boggy Creek*.

106. *Smoke in the Wind,* which was filmed in Waldron in 1971, was Walter Brennan's last picture. He was the Real McCoy.

AMAZING ARKANSAS

107. Archery great Ben Pearson was born in Paron on November 16, 1898, while today his home in Pine Bluff is on display. He was the first person in the world to mass produce hunting bows.

108. Jonesboro's Hattie W. Caraway became the first woman elected to a seat in the United States Senate in 1932. She was also the first woman chairman of a Senate committee, the first woman to conduct a Senate hearing and the first woman to preside over the Senate.

109. More than 50 percent of Arkansas is forest lands.

110. The opening scene of *Gone With the Wind* was of "the old mill" or Pugh's Mill, built in 1933, which still stands in North Little Rock at the corner of Fairway and Lakeshore Drive.

111. In 1976, Bill Clinton was elected Attorney General of Arkansas.

AMAZING ARKANSAS

112. The late knifemaker Jimmy Lile of Russellville designed and made all the knives used in the *Rambo* films. His shop, Jimmy Lile Handmade Knives, is still open for business. His knives are really sharp.

113. In 1972, the Buffalo River became the first official National River in the United States. About 85,000 people paddle their own canoe along the Buffalo River annually.

114. The first electric lights were switched on in Little Rock in September 1888 when 70 lights illuminated city streets.

115. The Arkansas Indian Culture Center and Folklore Museum is located in Hardy. Nearby is Cherokee Village, where there are 998 streets, from Ababich Lane to Zuni Circle, named after famous Native American tribes and their leaders.

116. The Arkansas State Mineral is quartz crystal.

AMAZING ARKANSAS

117. During the 1920s, Babe Ruth, Al Capone and his arch-enemy Bugs Moran spent part of their winters in Hot Springs, where they played the horses at Oaklawn Race Track. Capone always stayed at room 442 at the Arlington Hotel.

118. The levee at Arkansas City is the world's tallest, at 32 feet high, and longest, extending 1,608 miles along the Mississippi. You can drive your Chevy there if you wish.

119. Queen Wilhelmina State Park is the state's highest state park.

120. Greers Ferry Dam is the site of a "Do It If You Dare" cardboard boat race every year. The winner is the one whose cardboard boat floats the longest.

121. During the 1960s, Arnold Palmer's red, white and blue Super-Duper golf bag was made in Pocahontas by Kountry Klub of Arkansas.

AMAZING ARKANSAS

122. The Arkansas Travelers baseball team is Arkansas' only professional sports franchise. It is the double-A farm team of the St. Louis Cardinals. The Arkansas Travelers changed their name from the Little Rock Travelers in 1960.

123. John Patterson was the first white male born in Arkansas. Born in Marianna in 1790, his grave marker reads: "I was born in a Kingdom (Spain)/raised in an Empire (France)/attained manhood in a Territory (Arkansas)/and now am a citizen of a State/and have never been 100 miles from where I now live."

124. Best-selling author John Grisham (*The Firm, The Pelican Brief, A Time To Kill, The Client*) was born in Jonesboro on Feb. 8, 1955. He rebuffed the opportunity to run for the U.S. Senate in 1993 saying, "Senators are expected to shave and wear socks." You tell 'em, John.

125. The Arkansas State Gem is the diamond. I'll buy that.

AMAZING ARKANSAS

126. Potts Tavern in Pottsville was a stagecoach stop on the Butterfield Overland stage route. The stagecoach made a pot stop there.

127. Piggott's old Franklin Theater was the site of the world premiere of *A Farewell to Arms,* the 1933 movie starring Gary Cooper and Helen Hayes.

128. In the years 1864-1865, Arkansas had two state governments operating simultaneously, the Unionist government and the Confederate government. The Confederate capital of the state during the Civil War was Washington, Arkansas.

129. Arkansas is an Indian word for "downstream people." It was derived from the name of the Quapaw Indian tribe.

130. The most decorated Christmas house in the world is on Cantrell Street in Little Rock and has more than 1.5 million red lights. Stringing begins in September.

AMAZING ARKANSAS

131. The Arkansas legislature created the White River Monster Sanctuary and Retreat in 1973 in response to several sightings of the White River Monster. The bill says "No monster may be molested, killed or trampled."

132. Mountain View is called "the Folk Music Capital of the World" and is home of the Ozark Folk Center.

133. Arkansas has a patented apple, the Quindell, which is a cross between a Red Delicious and an Old-Fashioned Winesap. It was developed in 1942 in Green Forest by Ralph Banta. Quindell means "queen of the delicious." At the St. Louis World's Fair of 1904, Arkansas apples won all the top prizes and more than 200 medals. I'll bite that.

134. The most famous building on the campus of the University of Arkansas in Fayetteville is the twin-towered Old Main, which was built in 1875. It now houses the Fulbright College of Arts and Sciences.

AMAZING ARKANSAS

135. Bill Clinton taught law at the University of Arkansas in Fayetteville for two years.

136. Remington Arms in Lonoke is the sole producer of all the ammunition sold by Remington, America's oldest maker of sporting firearms.

137. Because of the talents of Mrs. Harry King, during the 1940s Batesville was recognized as "the Hooked Rug Capital" of the world. She later wrote a book on designs that became known as "the Bible" of hooked rugs.

138. Baseball Hall of Fame's Jerome Hanna "Dizzy" Dean was born in Lucas on January 16, 1911. The St. Louis Cardinal pitching ace from "the gashouse gang" era and his brother Paul "Daffy" Dean once combined to pitch a one-hit doubleheader. And "that's all she wrote, Pee Wee."

139. As a teen, Bill Clinton drove a 1961 Buick.

AMAZING ARKANSAS

140. The Concert Vineyards Winery at Lakeview grows 200 varieties of grapes on 18 acres, including the Cynthiana, a native Arkansas grape.

141. The heaviest twins to ever survive birth were born to Mrs. J.P. Haskin in Fort Smith on February 20, 1924. Their total weight was 27 pounds, 12 ounces.

142. Drive-in movie critic Joe Bob Briggs graduated from Little Rock's Central High but also studied for many hours at the Twin City Drive-In. There is no truth to the rumor that he is stoop-shouldered from spending so much time in automobile trunks.

143. In Hot Springs in 1902, H.I. Campbell began what was probably the first alligator farm in America. Today there are more than 250 gators at the farm, and the late "Pine Bluff" was said to be about 125 years old at the time of his death. There are an estimated 3,000-3,500 alligators in Arkansas today. See ya later, Arkie gator.

AMAZING ARKANSAS

144. Although Lonoke is the county seat of Lonoke County, Benton is not even in Benton County; nor is Searcy in Searcy County. In fact, Washington is not in Washington County, Van Buren is not in Van Buren County, Conway is not in Conway County, Marion is not in Marion County, Hot Springs is not in Hot Spring County, and, of course, Mississippi is not in Mississippi County.

145. Mammoth Spring in northwest Arkansas is one of the largest freshwater springs in the world with 216 million gallons gushing forth from it daily.

146. The TV show *Evening Shade* took its name from Evening Shade, Arkansas. The title was suggested by first lady Hillary Clinton.

147. At one time Arkansas produced 97 percent of the nation's bauxite ore, which is used in making aluminum. The mineral was discovered in Arkansas in 1887 by a state geologist.

AMAZING ARKANSAS

148. Country music's "Man in Black," Johnny Cash, was born in Kingsland on February 26, 1932.

149. "The Arkansas Philosopher" Bob Burns, a popular vaudeville, radio and film comedian who was born in Van Buren, invented the musical bazooka. Later, the military's famed bazooka gun was named after the instrument as was a popular brand of bubble gum.

150. Patsy Montana, who was born in Hot Springs on October 30, 1914, has been called the "Queen of Country Music." She became the first woman in country music to sell a million records with her 1935 hit *I Want To Be a Cowboy's Sweetheart*.

151. This sister couldn't spare a dime. In 1936, Mady Armstrong built a small house in Searcy with the 13,000 dimes that she saved from washing clothes and performing odd jobs over a ten-year period. "The Mistress of the Dime House" was featured in *Ripley's Believe It or Not* syndicated column that year.

AMAZING ARKANSAS

152. The Wolf House in Norfolk served as a post office, courthouse, stage and steamboat stop for more than 50 years. The two-story log cabin, built in the dog-trot style, is said to be the oldest in the state.

153. The Arkansas State Rock is bauxite. Constructed of bauxite boulders, Benton's Gann House is the world's only bauxite house. The wise man built his house upon the rock in 1893.

154. Davy Crockett once said, "If I could rest anywhere, it would be in the heart of Arkansas."

155. The Arkansas State Insect is the honeybee. Hmm.

156. Blind salamanders and albino crawdads can be found in one of the world's most beautiful caves, Arkansas' Blanchard Springs Caverns. The colorful cave has a touring trail 1.2 miles long.

157. The Arkansas State Flower is the apple blossom.

AMAZING ARKANSAS

158. If you remove all the "t's" from the town of Stuttgart, you have the word sugar, thus Stuttgart is also called Sugartown.

159. World-class Egyptian-Arabian horses are bred at the Ansata Arabian Stud Farm near Mena.

160. Ben Murphy, who starred in the TV western/comedy *Alias Smith and Jones,* was born in Jonesboro on March 6, 1941.

161. As a teen, Bill Clinton and his friends hung out at the Polar Bear drive-in in Hot Springs. Today it's called Bailey's Dairy Treat.

162. Eureka Springs is built around 63 springs, and all of the downtown area is listed on the National Register of Historic Places. I found it!

163. Bill Clinton went to pre-school at Miss Marie Purkins' School for Little Folks in Hope.

AMAZING ARKANSAS

164. Arkansas' nickname used to be "the Bear State" because of its large population of bears. The Game and Fish Commission released 250 black bears in the state during the 1960s. Now the black bear population is estimated to be about 2,500.

165. Frank Bonner, who starred as salesman Herb Tarlek on TV's *WKRP in Cincinnati,* was born in Little Rock on February 28, 1942.

166. The annual amount of rainfall in Arkansas is 49 inches.

167. Forget Jurassic Park, the world's largest dinosaur park is Dinosaur World near Eureka Springs. The 65-acre park contains a four-story tall King Kong.

168. Little Rock's "Geese" Ausbie, the "clown prince of basketball," and El Dorado native Reece "Goose" Tatum, were both stars for the Harlem Globetrotters. Ausbie also co-starred in 1981's *The Harlem Globetrotters on Gilligan's Island.*

AMAZING ARKANSAS

169. Actress Gail Davis, who starred as TV's Annie Oakley, was born in Little Rock on October 5, 1925.

170. Little Rock's original name was La Petit Roche, given to it by the explorer LaHarpe.

171. Berryville's Cosmic Cavern boasts the world's largest underground bridge. It also contains a geological formation that resembles Santa Claus. Ho-Ho-Hole.

172. Bill Clinton was ranked fourth academically in his high school class of 323 students.

173. The *King Biscuit Time* radio show has been broadcast on KFFA in Helena since November 1941. They're still playing the blues Monday through Friday.

174. Pine Bluff is home to the Arkansas Railroad Museum.

175. The Walton family of Wal-Mart fame was worth $23.8 billion in 1992.

AMAZING ARKANSAS

176. The cement Rainbow Arch Bridge at Cotter has five rainbow stands. It was built in 1930 for a half a million dollars.

177. In 1783, Arkansas Post was attacked by Captain James Colbert and his band of pirates, where they killed two men.

178. The Arkansas State Vegetable is the south Arkansas vine-ripened pink tomato – home-grown are best, of course.

179. John Hemphill's salt works was the first industry in Arkansas. It opened for business in 1814 in Blakeleytown.

180. In 1939, Helen Keller spoke at the dedication ceremony of a new building in Little Rock for the Arkansas School for the Blind.

181. Soybeans are Arkansas' most valuable farm product.

AMAZING ARKANSAS

182. Jack Stephens of Stephens Inc. in Little Rock is the chairman of the Masters golf tournament at Augusta, Georgia.

183. Little Rock's nickname was once "the city of Roses." Its nickname today is "the city full of suprises."

184. William Grant Still, one of America's outstanding 20th-century composers, was raised in Little Rock and was the first African-American to direct a major U.S. symphony orchestra (the Los Angeles Philharmonic) in 1936. He also wrote the theme music for the 1939 Chicago World's Fair.

185. The footpath to the top of the 1,001-foot high Sugar Loaf Mountain was the first National Nature Trail established by Congress. Take a hike.

186. President Bill Clinton was first elected governor of Arkansas at the age of 32 and served five terms for a total of 12 years as governor.

AMAZING ARKANSAS

187. DeGray Lake Resort State Park hosts an Owl Prowl on summer nights. They really give a hoot.

188. In 1929, 13-year-old Alice Taylor found a round stone the size of a quail's egg while chopping cotton in a field near Holly Springs. She kept it as a plaything until years later when her own children lost it through a hole in the floor. The stone was rediscovered while looking for eggs one day, and then, in 1942, she took it to a drugstore on the Searcy town square. Eventually the rock wound up at Tiffany's in New York, and Alice got a check for $8,500. The pretty rock proved to be a 27-carat diamond, the third largest ever found in North America.

189. Bill Clinton's senior class of 1964 held its prom in Hot Springs' Arlington Hotel.

190. Ed Walker's Drive-in in Fort Smith is probably the only place to offer curbside beer service in the U.S. Fill 'er up, Ed.

AMAZING ARKANSAS

191. The Arkansas Air Museum, "The Museum That Flies," is located at Drake Field in Fayetteville.

192. Hope is home of the world's largest watermelons, including a 200-pounder grown in 1980. Pass the salt.

193. "The Great Raft," a huge 100-mile log jam on Arkansas and Louisiana's Red River which impeded navigation until 1838, was so thickly clogged that men could ride across it on horseback. The log jam had been gelling for five hundred years.

194. Shelley Winters starred as Ma Barker in Roger Corman's *Bloody Mama,* which was filmed in Batesville in 1969. Robert De Niro and Bruce Dern were there also as two of Ma's boys.

195. The first newspaper to publish in the state was the *Arkansas Gazette*. Begun on November 20, 1819, it was the oldest paper west of the Mississippi at the time of its demise in October 1991.

AMAZING ARKANSAS

196. The first radio station in Arkansas was WOK, which began transmitting in February 1922 in Pine Bluff. The WOK stood for "worker of kilowatts."

197. Malvern is the brick capital of the world and produces more bricks than any other town. It is home to the Acme Brick Company and hosts an annual Brickfest with a brick-throwing contest. Ernest T. Bass need not apply.

198. Country music singer Barbara Fairchild was born in Knobel on November 12, 1950. She had a No. 1 hit in 1972 with the *Teddy Bear Song*.

199. Elvis Presley entertained in a local tavern in Newport in the 1950s. It was one for the money.

200. El Dorado's Rialto Theater is the only working art deco theater in the state.

201. Arkansas has 12,750 bridges.

AMAZING ARKANSAS

202. Arkansas is within 500 miles of one-third of the United States' population. From Little Rock it is 1,041 miles to Washington, D.C., 1,273 miles to New York City and 1,725 miles to Los Angeles.

203. Madame Tussaud's Wax Museum in Hot Springs was founded by the granddaughter of the famous Josephine Tussaud of London's famed museum. Be sure and see the young Elvis immortalized in wax.

204. Anderson's Minnow Farm in Lonoke, with more than 6,000 acres and 200 miles of levees, is the largest baitfish minnow farm in the world. Nibble on that.

205. Arkansas' John Gould Fletcher won the Pulitzer Prize for poetry in 1939 for his book *Selected Poems*.

206. From Searcy, Arkansas, it is possible to find Romance by going west on Pleasure Street and following the road through Joy, Harmony and Rose Bud.

AMAZING ARKANSAS

207. Advertised on a postcard in the 1940s as "the largest gas station in the world," the 555 Building stood at Third and Broadway in Little Rock and displayed a Model-T Ford on the roof, which was considered an engineering marvel of its time.

208. The area around Mount Ida is known as the "Quartz Crystal Capital of the World."

209. Palarm Creek near Mayflower is the geographical center of Arkansas.

210. The three-story Queen Wilhelmina Lodge, known as "the Castle in the Sky," was originally built atop Rich Mountain in 1898. It was named for the queen of Holland by Dutch investors who hoped she would visit the inn.

211. Arkansas state nicknames include "The Bear State," "Land of Opportunity," "The Wonder State" and "The Natural State."

AMAZING ARKANSAS

212. The original "MacArthur Park" is in Little Rock, the birthplace of Gen. Douglas MacArthur. He was born there on January 26, 1880, and the Museum of Science and History is also located there.

213. Hog Heaven, a store in Texarkana, features razorback items of every type, even razorback toilet seats. Ouch!

214. Gen. William O. Darby, the leader of Darby's Rangers of World War II fame, grew up in Fort Smith.

215. Sonny Liston, who won the heavyweight boxing crown of the world from Floyd Patterson on September 25, 1962, was born in Forrest City on May 8, 1932, one of his father's 25 children.

216. Arkansas' Felsenthal National Wildlife Refuge is the world's largest green-tree reservoir and is home to alligators, bald eagles and red-cockaded woodpeckers. The latter knock on wood.

AMAZING ARKANSAS

217. The post office clerk in Romance spends practically all day on Valentine's Day stamping postmarks on letters from across the United States. On Valentine's Day 1991, the Postmaster General of the United States visited Romance to unveil a special "Love" postage stamp. To celebrate the big occasion, several couples were wed in the Romance Church of Christ. How sweet it is.

218. The motto on Arkansas license plates is "The Natural State," naturally.

219. The oldest national cemetery in the United States is located in Fort Smith, and is the burial place of Judge Isaac Parker. R.I.P.

220. Little Rock got its name from a rock on the south side of the Arkansas River which was compared to a huge rock farther upriver on the north side. Fort Roots Hospital was built on the big rock in North Little Rock.

AMAZING ARKANSAS

221. Arkansas provides pachyderms a playground. Old and injured elephants are cared for at Riddle's Elephant Breeding Farm and Wildlife Sanctuary. The elephants even have a 2,000-yard "swimming pool."

222. Arkansas averages 20 tornadoes per year, most frequently in the month of April. About 817 tornadoes have hit the state over the last 40 years.

223. The 48-feet tall glass chapel of Thorncrown Chapel, near Eureka Springs, has been called "the most beautiful little chapel in the world" and contains more than 6,000 square feet of glass in the walls and skylight. Mama don't allow no rock throwing around here.

224. In 1921, El Dorado prospered with the discovery of oil. Four years later, oil millionaire H.L. Hunt got his start in the business here speculating in the Arkansas oil fields and became one of the richest men in the world.

AMAZING ARKANSAS

225. A gallows was once built in Fort Smith to hang 12 men simultaneously. That's stretching it a bit.

226. The University of Alabama's legendary coach Paul "Bear" Bryant, was born in Moro Bottom near Fordyce on September 11, 1913. He was an All-State football player for the Fordyce Redbugs and picked up his nickname after wrestling a bear on a dare when he was a teen-ager.

227. The average temperature in Arkansas in the winter is 42 degrees. The average temperature in Arkansas in the summer is 79 degrees.

228. Scenes of the 1970 film *Two Lane Blacktop* were shot in Arkansas with singer James Taylor and Warren Oates as two drivers racing GTOs across the South.

229. Dr. Charles McDermott, who settled Dermott, received a patent for a flying machine in 1872.

AMAZING ARKANSAS

230. Arkansas' Bayou Bartholomew is the longest bayou in the world at 333 miles long. The bayou crosses into Louisiana.

231. Before he was scratched from the lineup at the I.Q. Zoo in Hot Springs, there was a baseball-playing chicken named Chicky Mantle. He always hit fowl balls. Boo. Chicky was replaced by Elvis, the guitar-playing duck. The I.Q. Zoo is now known as the Educated Animal Zoo.

232. During his 1992 appearance on *The Arsenio Hall Show,* Bill Clinton played *Heartbreak Hotel* on his saxophone.

233. The first TV station in Arkansas was KRTV, which began operating April 5, 1953, in Little Rock.

234. National baby and child-care expert Dr. Benjamin Spock lived for many years near Rogers, Arkansas.

AMAZING ARKANSAS

235. The boundaries of Arkansas, Oklahoma and Missouri meet at Three Corners and are marked by three stones dating from 1821 to the 1960s. There is only one other place in the U.S. that has more converging state lines.

236. The first mail route in Arkansas started on January 19, 1815, from St. Louis. In 1851, mail sent from California to Arkansas came by way of Cape Horn to New York to Arkansas.

237. The National Lum & Abner Society hosts its annual convention on the Saturday following Father's Day each year in Mena, Arkansas, the town where Chet Lauck (Lum) and Norris Goff (Abner) first met as boys and grew up. Lauck was born in Alleene in 1902 and Goff was born in Cove in 1906. By doggies.

238. Singer/actor William Warfield (*Showboat, Porgy and Bess*) was born in West Helena on June 20, 1920.

AMAZING ARKANSAS

239. The only way to get to Sugar Loaf Mountain is by boat. It's on an island in the middle of Greers Ferry Lake.

240. Crawford County's courthouse, the oldest active courthouse west of the Mississippi, boasts a Seth Thomas courthouse clock that has been chiming the hours since October 15, 1887, even though the hands of the clock do not turn.

241. Arkansas became a part of the United States under President Thomas Jefferson through the Louisiana Purchase in 1803. The Arkansas Territory was purchased at a price of three cents per acre, which means the entire state cost just under a million dollars. And you think you got a good deal at that garage sale last Saturday.

242. The Arkansas State Motto is *regnat populus* – "Let the people rule."

AMAZING ARKANSAS

243. A beaver weighing 156 pounds was trapped in Arkansas and displayed in Little Rock on January 8, 1880. Gnaw on that for a while.

244. Piano man Floyd Cramer of *Last Date* fame grew up in Huttig. He studied piano in El Dorado under Mrs. Stanley Anderson.

245. In 1904, when there were about four automobiles in Little Rock, the speed limit was eight miles per hour in town and 15 miles per hour outside the city limits.

246. In 1972, Little Rock was designated a foreign trade zone, one of only two at the time located in inland ports.

247. Bill Clinton is allergic to dust, milk, chocolate, weed and grass pollen and cat dander. Sorry about that, Socks.

AMAZING ARKANSAS

248. Hall of Fame baseball star Lou Brock was born in El Dorado on June 18, 1939. The fleet St. Louis Cardinal once held the major league career base-stealing record.

249. Winthrop Rockefeller built the Museum of Automobiles atop Petit Jean Mountain. Among the vehicles on display is Mae West's pink Packard. Why don't you come up and see it some time?

250. Poet/author Maya Angelou grew up in Stamps. She read her poem *A Little Lower Than the Angels* for Bill Clinton's inauguration, and is the author of *I Know Why the Caged Bird Sings*.

251. Fuller's Earth was first discovered in the United States in Benton, Arkansas, in 1891 by John Olson. Look it up in the encyclopedia.

AMAZING ARKANSAS

252. The notch in the northeast corner of the state was due to an influential landowner, Col. John H. Walker, who, rather than have his land extend across two state borders, sought to have all of his land retained in the New Madrid District or "bootheel" of Missouri.

253. Has Owens of Scarcy was one of the world's largest mule dealers, and during World War II sold more mules to the United States Army than any other man. In one year alone, Owens sold more than 2,000 mules at about $70 apiece. That's a lot of jack.

254. The only diamond mine in the United States is in Murfreesboro, Arkansas. For $4 you can have a gem dandy day in the 80-acre Crater of Diamonds State Park and any diamond you find is yours. More than 70,000 diamonds have been found there, including the 40-carat "Uncle Sam" diamond which was discovered in 1924.

AMAZING ARKANSAS

255. In the 1960s, there was a soda pop named after the Arkansas Razorback football team. It was called Red Hog, and if you drank too much you were a Red Hog hog. Another famous Arkansas soft drink was Grapette, which was originated by B.F. Fooks of Camden in 1926 when he traded his gas station for a bottling plant. Grapette was one of the most popular beverages in the U.S. with more than 600 bottling plants in 38 states. The company motto was "Drink Grapette, my friend." Then there's this other soft drink known as Sam's Cola.

256. The lowest point in the state, 54 feet above sea level, is at the Ouachita River near the Louisiana border.

257. To enter St. Elizabeth's Catholic Church in Eureka Springs, visitors must enter through the top of the bell tower. Don't bump your head or your ears will ring.

AMAZING ARKANSAS

258. Orval Faubus was elected to six consecutive terms as governor of Arkansas, from 1955-1967.

259. In 1991, the *Arkansas Gazette* asked three noted state historians to select the twenty most important Arkansans of the 20th century. Their choices were: businessman Sam Walton, poet Maya Angelou, architect Fay Jones, politician Orval Faubus, evangelist Ben Bogard, activist Daisy Bates, businessman Witt Stephens, coach Frank Broyles, politician Winthrop Rockefeller, politician Hattie Caraway, politician Jeff Davis, conductor William Grant Still, politician Charles Brough, poet John Gould Fletcher, politician Brooks Hays, educator Robert W. Leflar, politician Joe T. Robinson, politician J. William Fulbright, politician Wilbur Mills and newspaper editor J.N. Heiskill.

260. Bill Clinton's presidential campaign theme song was *Don't Stop* by Fleetwood Mac.

AMAZING ARKANSAS

261. From the years 1903-1904, the University of Arkansas football team played games against Fort Smith High School.

262. On their way to Texas, Davy Crockett, Jim Bowie, Stephen Austin and Sam Houston took the Southwest Trail through Arkansas. Sam Houston reportedly recruited men and plotted the Texas revolution at a tavern in Washington. Remember the Alamo!

263. Gil Gerard, star of TV's *Buck Rogers in the 25th Century*, was born in Little Rock on January 23, 1943.

264. Guns belonging to Billy the Kid, Annie Oakley, Jesse James, Pancho Villa, Buffalo Bill, Sam Houston and Wild Bill Hickok can be seen at the Saunders Memorial Museum in Berryville. Aw, shoot.

265. The Arkansas State Bird is the mockingbird. Listen.

AMAZING ARKANSAS

266. Pine Bluff annually hosts the King Cotton Holiday Basketball Classic, the top high school basketball tournament in the nation, according to *The New York Times*.

267. Arkansas is No. 1 in the nation in producing farm chickens, turkeys and broilers (chickens between nine and 12 weeks old).

268. Country music's "Silver Fox" Charlie Rich was born behind closed doors in Colt, near Forrest City, on December 14, 1932.

269. "On Christmas Day, 1918, every one of the more than two million American soldiers in France received a pound box of chocolate candy, bearing the inscription, 'Made from sugar saved by the women of the State of Arkansas out of their allotment'," wrote former Arkansas Governor Brough in a letter to H.L. Mencken and the *Baltimore Sun*.

AMAZING ARKANSAS

270. The Corn Cob Inn, a bed-and-breakfast place in Everton, was once a corncob pipe factory. Put that in your pipe and smoke it.

271. Bill Clinton's 1967 light blue Mustang convertible is on display at the Museum of Automobiles on Petit Jean Mountain. He bought it from his brother Roger.

272. *Little Rock* was a No. 1 country hit for Reba McEntire in 1986.

273. Arkansas' first city and first state capital was Arkansas Post. It was established in 1686 by the French explorer Henri de Tonti, who has been called "the Father of Arkansas."

274. Oklahoma humorist and cowboy Will Rogers was married in Rogers to Betty Blake on November 25, 1906. Will said, "When I roped her – that was the star performance of my life."

AMAZING ARKANSAS

275. At 550 feet and 41 stories high, the tallest building in Arkansas is the TCBY Building in Little Rock. TCBY (The Country's Best Yogurt) is the world's largest franchiser, licensor and operator of retail stores specializing in frozen yogurt products with 1,840 locations in all of the fifty states and nine foreign countries. The first TCBY store was opened October 1, 1981, at 1840 Rodney Parham Road in Little Rock.

276. Zero Mountain, south of Springdale, has a cave which is artificially cooled and which can store almost 45 million pounds of food.

277. Stuttgart is called the "Rice and Duck Capital of the World."

278. Andy Griffith and Lee Remick made their film debuts in *A Face in the Crowd* in 1957, which was partly filmed in Piggott.

AMAZING ARKANSAS

279. None of the streets in Eureka Springs intersect at right angles. All right! Not!

280. Football Hall of Fame member Bobby Mitchell was born in Hot Springs on June 6, 1935.

281. In 1923, Elbert Fausett of Sheridan became the youngest Ford automobile dealer in the nation. The 19-year-old set up his shop in Hensley, Arkansas.

282. In the midst of Arkansas' Mississippi Delta rises a geographical oddity, Crowley's Ridge, which runs about 200 miles north to south in country which is otherwise flat.

283. Jazz musician Alphonso Trent of Fort Smith and his local group were the first black band to be broadcast in America by playing Big Band sounds in the 1920s and '30s.

AMAZING ARKANSAS

284. Arkansas was the twenty-fifth state admitted into the union in 1836.

285. Near Malvern, swans, emus and pheasants abound at the Feathered Nest Wildlife Farm.

286. The International Order of Hoo-Hoos Museum can be found in Gurdon. The Hoo-Hoos are a fraternity of lumbermen. When they attend baseball games, you can hear boo Hoo-Hoos.

287. Little Rock's Gen. Douglas MacArthur is considered the "Most Decorated American Soldier." He served in the Spanish-American War, World War I and World War II.

288. In 1993, Arkadelphia was listed in the book, *50 Fabulous Places to Raise Your Family.* The town is also known as the wildflower capital of Arkansas.

AMAZING ARKANSAS

289. Built in 1880, Wiederkehr Winery, atop St. Mary's Mountain, is the oldest and largest winery in mid-America. A restaurant there is located in the winery's original cellar.

290. The 1.6-million acre Ouachita National Forest, set aside by President Theodore Roosevelt in 1907, is the oldest and largest national forest in the South and covers nearly all of Montgomery County.

291. Three unrelated communities in Arkansas can be linked to form the name of the great poet/essayist Ralph Waldo Emerson.

292. Actor Laurence Luckinbill was born in Fort Smith on November 21, 1934. He is married to Lucie Arnaz, daughter of Lucille Ball and Desi Arnaz. "Lucie, I'm home."

AMAZING ARKANSAS

293. The first library in the state was built in 1843 in Little Rock.

294. The Arkansas Oil and Brine Museum in Smackover features a working oil well. Well.

295. Charles Portis, author of *True Grit,* was born in El Dorado on Dec. 28, 1933. The film version of the novel earned John Wayne his only Oscar as he portrayed Marshal Rooster Cogburn.

296. In 1909, Coach Hugo Bezdek changed the name of the University of Arkansas Cardinals to the Razorbacks.

297. Sonora Dodd, who was born in 1882 in Jenny Lind, Arkansas, founded Father's Day in 1910. She was definitely daddy's little girl.

AMAZING ARKANSAS

298. Clifton Clowers of Center Ridge, Arkansas, was the subject of the hit song *Wolverton Mountain,* which has sold over 20 million copies. It was written by his nephew, Merle Kilgore. Clowers turned 100 in 1991, and they still say "don't go on Wolverton Mountain."

299. One of Bill Clinton's favorite eating spots in Little Rock is Doe's Eat Place.

300. The Little Golden Gate Bridge at Beaver is a 528-foot steel cable suspension bridge that was built in 1947 and then painted gold. Only one automobile may cross at a time.

301. A one-ton block of marble from Harrison was sent to Washington, D.C., to be used in the Washington Monument.

302. The former Helena Union Train Depot is home to the Delta Cultural Center.

AMAZING ARKANSAS

303. The University of Arkansas track team has won ten consecutive NCAA indoor track titles under Coach John McDonnell.

304. Elton Britt, "King of the Yodelers," was born in Marshall on July 7, 1917. In 1944, his song, *There's a Star Spangled Banner Waving Somewhere,* became country music's first official gold record.

305. Circus elephants have always been popular in the state. The Schell Brothers Four Ring Circus of 1933 featured Baby Bolo, an elephant that could add, subtract and multiply, while the Seils-Sterling Circus, which toured the state in 1937, starred Billy Sunday, the oldest-living pachyderm in America. Billy had been performing in circuses since 1860. In 1943, the Dailey Brothers Circus went to bat across Arkansas with an elephant baseball game that was umpired by Norma Davenport, the world's youngest elephant trainer.

AMAZING ARKANSAS

306. Eureka Springs is the smallest city in America with a public trolley system.

307. Atop Rich Mountain stands an historical fire tower which rises 2,681 feet above the valley below.

308. Bentonville's Randy Ober holds the world record for spitting tobacco. He sent a wad flying 47-feet 7-inches at the fifth annual Calico Tobacco Chewing and Spitting Contest on April 4, 1982, in north California.

309. Country music singer and *80's Lady* K.T. Oslin was born in Crossett on May 15, 1942. The "K.T." stands for Kay Toinette.

310. Arkansas has historically been a one-party (Democratic) state, but in 1968, Arkansas voters elected a Republican governor (Rockefeller), a Democratic senator (Fulbright) and an independent candidate for president (George Wallace).

AMAZING ARKANSAS

311. At the Wegner Quartz Crystal Mines near Mount Ida you can dig for your own crystals. But you probably won't find Billy there.

312. The Italian community of Tontitown, Arkansas, hosts an annual Tontitown Grape Festival featuring handmade spaghetti and sauce. It's the oldest festival in the state. The town's historical museum has spaghetti machines on display.

313. The Arkansas state capitol building in Little Rock was modeled after the U.S. capitol in Washington, D.C.

314. The community of Ben Hur was named for the 1880 novel by Gen. Lew Wallace, but Charlton Heston has never been there.

315. Texarkana derives its name from three states – Texas, Arkansas and Louisiana.

AMAZING ARKANSAS

316. Country music singer Jim Ed Brown was born in Sparkman on April 1, 1934. He and his sisters, Maxine and Bonnie, had a No. 1 hit as the Browns in 1959 with *The Three Bells*.

317. The Gay Nineties Button and Doll Museum in Onyx Cave Park near Eureka Springs features a collection of 10,000 buttons.

318. A state record 215-pound alligator gar was caught with a minnow as bait on the Arkansas River near Dardanelle in 1964.

319. After Cabot's three-foot two-inch Lena Jones graduated from Galloway College, she joined the Golden Belt Show, thus becoming the only lady midget in show business with a college degree.

320. Bill Clinton's favorite Beatle is Paul McCartney.

AMAZING ARKANSAS

321. Diamond Cave in Jasper is a 21-mile long cave which used to be entered by pulling back a plastic shower curtain.

322. Barbara Hershey, David Carradine and Melinda Dillon starred in *Boxcar Bertha*, which was partly filmed in Camden in 1972. It was Martin Scorcese's directorial debut. Dillon was born in Hope and has twice been nominated for Oscars for her work in *Close Encounters of the Third Kind* and *Absence of Malice*.

323. Of the 13 meteorites found in Arkansas, six were seen when they fell, and the Paragould Meteorite, which fell on February 12, 1930, created a crater 8-feet-deep and 28 inches long. It came from outer space and weighed 408 kilograms. We don't know how much that is in pounds, but it was said to be one of the ten biggest meteorites in the world when it was sold to the Field Museum of Natural History in Chicago.

AMAZING ARKANSAS

324. A part of the little rock, from which Little Rock got its name, was blown away when construction crews were building a railroad bridge across the Arkansas River. The remainder of the "little rock" is marked by a bronze plaque.

325. The long-running *Lum & Abner* radio show (1931-1954) was set in Pine Ridge, Arkansas. On April 26, 1936, the community of Waters changed its name to Pine Ridge in honor of the show. Today, the Jot-Em-Down Store and Lum & Abner Museum are both located there.

326. Would you believe 50 million seedlings are born each year from 600 parent trees at the Weyerhaeuser Company Reforestation Center near Magnolia? I wood.

327. Arkansas has 2.4 million acres of national forestland.

AMAZING ARKANSAS

328. From 1980-1983, the Mississippi County Community College near Blytheville got its total energy requirements from the sun. A bright idea.

329. Mary Conway of Little Rock was named "beauty queen of the gold rush" after she rode horseback from Little Rock to California in 1850. Two Fayetteville women, the Fretschlag sisters, walked to California during the gold rush of 1849.

330. The Joe Logan Fish Hatchery in Lonoke is the world's largest government-owned fish hatchery with 267 acres. It is also the oldest warm-water hatchery in the nation.

331. The first telephone company in Arkansas was the Western-Union Telephone Exchange, which began November 1, 1879, in Little Rock with 40 subscribers. It was the third telephone exchange in the U.S. and had the country's first female operator, Kate Adams.

AMAZING ARKANSAS

332. Long-time University of Oklahoma Sooner football coach Barry Switzer was born in Crossett on October 5, 1937.

333. The Basin Park Hotel in Eureka Springs is built against the side of a mountain and each of the seven floors has access to a ground entrance.

334. Helen Gurley Brown, editor-in-chief of *Cosmopolitan* magazine, was born in Green Forest on February 18, 1922. You've come a long way, girley.

335. Carry A. Nation, women's sufferance and ax-wielding temperance advocate, made her last temperance speech in Eureka Springs and lived there from 1909 until her death.

336. The first Arkansas State Fair was held in 1867 and was called the State Agricultural and Mechanical Association.

AMAZING ARKANSAS

337. The Ouachita Hiking Trail at Pinnacle Mountain State Park stretches 225 miles to Talihena, Oklahoma. It is a National Recreation Trail.

338. Petit Jean Mountain was named after the legend of a French girl who disguised herself as a boy and traveled with her sailor sweetheart to America. A grave at the eastern end of the mountain marks her final resting place.

339. Oaklawn Park in Hot Springs opened in 1905 with the country's first glass-enclosed, steam-heated grandstand. It is the leading single tourist attraction in the state. I'll bet.

340. The W.G. Huxtable Pumping Plant in Marianna is one of the largest flood control facility's in the world and can pump 5.4 millions gallons of water per minute. That's a lot of water.

AMAZING ARKANSAS

341. A preacher built the foundation for his house with all but two tombstones from the Mount Pleasant Cemetery near Supply, Arkansas.

342. Arkansas is first in the production of Novaculite, which is used for making whetstones for sharpening knives. Never a dull moment.

343. At Pickles Gap near Conway, elephant rides are available some weekends for $3. That's not in peanuts either.

344. In 1983, three-foot-long tracks of the pleurocoelus, discovered in a gypsum mine near Nashville, were the first proof that dinosaurs once roamed Arkansas.

345. Approximately 23,000 World War II prisoners of war were interned at three locations in the state: Fort Chaffee, Fort Dermott and Camp Robinson.

AMAZING ARKANSAS

346. Approximately 46% of Arkansas' radio listeners tune in to country music.

347. The Christ of the Ozarks in Eureka Springs is a seven-story tall statue of Jesus which overlooks the Ozark Mountains.

348. The first circus to perform in Arkansas was Raymond and Waring's Great Zoological Exhibition of the City of New York on November 23, 1846.

349. At a park in Tontitown is the site of what is probably the only public boccie court in the country. Boccie anyone?

350. The Sesquicentennial Sun Dial at the foot of the Broadway Bridge in North Little Rock has a 40-foot square face and a 15-foot gnomon and is probably the largest horizontal sun dial in the world. I didn't gnome that.

AMAZING ARKANSAS

351. Bill Clinton took his surname from his stepfather, the late Roger Clinton, who operated a Buick dealership in Hot Springs.

352. From 1915 to 1920, Cass, Arkansas, reportedly produced more wooden wagon wheels than any place in the world. The place was well-spoken for.

353. Arkansas is the only state mentioned in the Bible. In Genesis it reads, "Noah looked out of the ark and saw."

354. The Arkansas City Methodist Church, built in 1889 facing Kate Adams Avenue, was turned ninety degrees by a tornado to face a different direction, toward Capital Street.

355. The only federal building that is on the border of two states, a post office in Texarkana, is built out of Texas granite and Arkansas limestone.

AMAZING ARKANSAS

356. The 10 most-populated cities in Arkansas are: 1) Little Rock, 175,795; 2) Fort Smith, 72,798; 3) North Little Rock, 61,741; 4) Pine Bluff, 57,140; 5) Jonesboro, 46,535; 6) Fayetteville, 42,099; 7) Hot Springs, 32,462; 8) Springdale, 29,941; 9) Jacksonville, 29,101; and 10) West Memphis, 28,259. The total population of the state is 2,395,000, give or take a few.

357. Country music star Conway Twitty took his first name from the town of Conway, Arkansas. The late singer had more No. 1 songs than any other artist and grew up in Helena under the name of Harold Jenkins.

358. Lepanto hosts an annual Terrapin Derby on the first Saturday in October. No hares allowed.

359. Jim Dandy Mangrum, leader of the rock group Black Oak Arkansas, is from Black Oak, Arkansas. There are two Black Oaks in the state.

AMAZING ARKANSAS

360. Little Rock's Fannie Turner passed her written exam for a driver's license in October 1978. It was her 104th attempt.

361. Charles "Boss" Schmidt, born in Coal Hill, Arkansas, on September 12, 1880, and a catcher for the Detroit Tigers, was reportedly the only ballplayer to defeat Ty Cobb in a fair battle of fisticuffs.

362. Three recent Arkansas governors now reside in Washington, D.C.: Dale Bumpers and David Pryor in the U.S. Senate and Bill Clinton in the White House.

363. The 1981 miniseries *The Blue and the Gray* was shot in Van Buren and at Prairie Grove State Park. It featured University of Arkansas athletic director Frank Broyles, who in a thick Southern accent announced, "Gentlemen, the President is dead." (Of course, the word "dead" had two syllables.)

AMAZING ARKANSAS

364. Among the items Bill Clinton has collected are duck calls, campaign buttons and bowie knives, and, oh, yes, votes.

365. Chelsea Victoria Clinton was born February 27, 1980, at Baptist Medical Center in Little Rock and weighed six pounds and one and three-fourths ounces. Her name was inspired by the 1960s Judy Collins song *It Was a Chelsea Morning.* Chelsea is also a New York City park.

366. Pivot Rock in Eureka Springs is about 15 feet tall, 30 feet in circumference at the top and 16 inches at the base. Go ahead, try to push it over.

367. When the 1985 TV movie *Under Siege* was filmed in Little Rock, the state capitol's dome was accidentally scorched during the shooting.

AMAZING ARKANSAS

368. Jimmy Driftwood, who was born in Mountain View on June 20, 1917, wrote *The Battle of New Orleans* to teach a history lesson to his students in 1936. It became a smash hit for Johnny Horton in 1959. Driftwood also wrote *Tennessee Stud.*

369. Approximately 99 of every 100 Arkansans were born in the United States.

370. On the grounds of the now defunct Citadel Bible College in Ozark is a two-story log house built with logs from every state.

371. The world's largest greyhound racing facility is Southland Greyhound Park in West Memphis. Doggonitt.

372. The world-famous Klipsch Speakers are made in Oakhaven, about four miles from Hope.

AMAZING ARKANSAS

373. When Lepanto was founded as a town, the only way in was by boat on the Little River. In Lepanto, the Rivervale Tunnel was built beneath one river for another one to flow through, so the two rivers cross.

374. The DeQueen newspaper is called *DeQueen Bee*. Get it? The queen bee?

375. Jim Bowie's famous Bowie Knife was designed by blacksmith James Black in Washington, Arkansas, in about 1825. The story goes that soon afterwards, Bowie was attacked by three desperadoes and killed them with his knife. The legend is that when Bowie died at the Alamo, the knife was in his hands. The single-edged blade was from 10 to 15 inches long and was also nicknamed "the Arkansas toothpick."

376. Bill Clinton jogs an average of four miles a day, six days a week.

AMAZING ARKANSAS

377. There are two free state ferry boats operated daily in Arkansas: the Spring Bank ferry, which crosses the Red River, and the Peel Ferry, which crosses Bull Shoals Lake.

378. The world's No. 1 outdoor drama, *The Great Passion Play* in Eureka Springs, depicts Christ's last week on earth, and almost 200 townspeople work as actors in it. More than five million people have seen the play.

379. At Classic Candies in Ratcliff you can take a bite of Arkansas. The candy makers offer a chocolate almond bar with the outline of Arkansas impressed upon it. It costs $1.50.

380. Arkansas has 541 miles of interstate highways.

381. An oil well drilled in El Dorado in 1921 blew so big that it rained oil more than two miles away. "Oil's well that ends well."

AMAZING ARKANSAS

382. Bill Clinton's favorite book is *War and Peace.*

383. When the nine-foot wide Dollarway Road to Pine Bluff was finished in 1914, it was the longest stretch of concrete pavement in the nation at 23.6 miles. It cost about a dollar per linear foot to build.

384. Hit country singer Tracy Lawrence was raised in Foreman and truly made No. 1 with a bullet. He completed the vocals to his hit song *Sticks and Stones* on May 31, 1991, and was shot that night on Nashville's Music Row. He still carries the bullet in his body.

385. Batesville is the oldest city in the state.

386. Arkansas' first gas street lights illuminated Little Rock in 1860. They were lit at dusk and snuffed at dawn by Benjamin Pate and Richard Wilson.

AMAZING ARKANSAS

387. Arkansas lobsters, actually crawdads, are exported to as far away as Peru in South America and Saudi Arabia in the Middle East.

388. The National Fish Hatchery in Heber Springs produces almost a million trout annually to stock waters in Arkansas and Texas.

389. President John F. Kennedy dedicated the Greer's Ferry Dam on October 3, 1963, a month before his assassination. In 1984, a tornado coming down the Little Red River destroyed the lake's Edgemont Bridge.

390. John Harold Johnson, the publisher of *Jet* and *Ebony* magazines, was born in Arkansas City on January 19, 1918.

391. Miracle Mansion in Eureka Springs has the world's oldest bug collection. Don't let it bug you.

AMAZING ARKANSAS

392. President Bill Clinton's Secret Service code name was Eagle while he ran for the nation's top political office. His brother Roger's code name was Headache. Have you tried B.C.?

393. Pottsville is home to one of the only two hat museums in the United States.

394. Hazel Walker, who played basketball for Ashdown High School in the early 1930s, was one of the greatest women basketball players of all time. At 5-feet 8-inches tall, she was an All-American 11 times as an amateur. She formed her own team, the Arkansas Travelers, and from 1949-1965 the squad played mostly against male teams and won 80 percent of their games. At halftime Hazel would put on a free throw exhibition by shooting 15 shots standing up, 10 from her knees and five while sitting on the floor, and she usually sank every one of the shots. After retiring, she made a quilt from her old uniforms.

AMAZING ARKANSAS

395. The great flood of 1927 covered almost one fourth of the state. While the waters rose in Pine Bluff, 500 people, stranded on a bridge, sang *We Shall Gather at the River*. Two births and two deaths occurred on a bridge near Pine Bluff during the night of April 22, 1927, where 35 people fled to escape "the great flood of '27."

396. A 1936 book lists the seven natural wonders of Arkansas as Hot Springs, Mammoth Spring, Diamond Cave, Mount Magazine, Magnet Cove, the Diamond Mine and the Bauxite mines.

397. Margaret Neel of Searcy gave Betty Grable a run for her money. The volunteer nurse served in India during World War II and was selected as the International Red Cross Poster Girl. Her face was seen on more than one million, four hundred thousand posters.

398. The Arkansas State Beverage is milk. I'll drink to that.

AMAZING ARKANSAS

399. On April 15, 1880, Ulysses S. Grant became the first man who had ever been president to visit Arkansas. Grant County was named after the Civil War hero and politician.

400. Pine Bluff is the second-oldest town in Arkansas. Barraque Street in Pine Bluff was the first paved street in the state.

401. New Subiaco Abbey, an academy built between 1898 and 1927 by Benedictine monks in Paris, Arkansas, is the only monastery in the state. It has a museum that contains a 1673 edition of *Don Quixote De La Mancha* and several hundred salt and pepper shakers.

402. The first theatrical performance given in Arkansas took place in Little Rock on November 4, 1834, and was a comedy called *Soldier's Daughter*.

AMAZING ARKANSAS

403. As a youth, Bill Clinton went to the movies at Hot Springs' Malco Theater.

404. In the early 1800s, Little Rock changed its name to Arkopolis. They soon dropped it because nobody used it.

405. For many years the tombstone of Salem founder lawyer William P. Morris could be found in a closet in the Salem courthouse. In the late 1980s, the tombstone was moved to the courthouse lawn.

406. Five-time Grammy winner Glen Campbell was born in Delight on April 22, 1935. The singing star made his film debut in fellow Arkansan Charles Portis' *True Grit*. Glen is a delightful fellow.

407. The Mt. Olive Methodist Church in Van Buren is believed to be the oldest black church west of the Mississippi.

AMAZING ARKANSAS

408. Little Rock's Quapaw Quarter, a housing district dating to the 1840s, has 135 buildings listed in the National Registry of Historic Places.

409. For five months in 1925, Smackover was the largest oil field in the United States. A 112-foot wooden derrick, built in the early 1920s at Smackover's Oil Field Park, is the tallest wooden derrick structure in the world.

410. Two Olympic triple-jump gold medalists hail from Arkansas universities: 1984-winner Al Joyner attended Arkansas State University, and 1992-winner Mike Conley attended the University of Arkansas. That's some feet.

411. Arkansas has 9,700 miles of rivers and streams and 600,000 acres of lakes. Water, water everywhere.

AMAZING ARKANSAS

412. The 1976 film *9-30-55* was filmed in Conway with Richard Thomas starring as a young man deeply affected by the death of movie star James Dean. It was directed by the late Arkansan James Bridges who was a college student in Conway at the time of Dean's death. Film director and screenwriter Bridges, who worked on such films as *The Paper Chase, The China Syndrome* and *Urban Cowboy,* was born in Little Rock on February 2, 1936, and grew up in Paris, Arkansas.

413. Bill and Hillary Clinton were wed October 11, 1975, in a home wedding at Fayetteville. Bill's first words to Hillary were: "We grow the world's largest watermelons in Arkansas." With that smooth line, how could she resist.

414. Miss Laura's Social Club in Fort Smith is the only bordello on the National Register of Historic Places.

AMAZING ARKANSAS

415. Sonny Boy Williamson, the musician who was responsible for the acceptance of the harmonica as an authentic blues instrument, spent the last years of his life in Helena.

416. Boston Braves pitching ace Johnny Sain was born in Havana on November 25, 1917. He was half of the mound duo made famous by the saying "Spahn and Sain and pray for rain."

417. The Trail of Tears passes through northern Arkansas, and Sequoyah wrote part of the Cherokee alphabet while in the state.

418. Football Hall of Fame's Don Hutson was born in Pine Bluff on Jan. 31, 1913. He led the NFL five times in scoring and eight seasons in pass receiving. At one time, he and Bear Bryant were the starting offensive ends for the Alabama Crimson Tide.

AMAZING ARKANSAS

419. Dee Brown, author of *Bury My Heart at Wounded Knee,* is a graduate of Little Rock's Central High and State College of Arkansas.

420. The 1920s ragtime song *Ding Dong Daddy From Dumas* is believed to have been inspired by a male dancer and has since become the Dumas, Arkansas, theme song and inspiration for its annual festival.

421. Mayor Frank Headlee went on a Little Rock television program in 1954 to promote Searcy. He claimed the town was rich, and then quoted the following words: "Every blade of grass has a green bulk, every bird has a bill, the chimneys have their drafts, every house has a check, every ditch has two banks, the streets were flushed, the lawns get a rake off, the clouds have a silver lining, and every flower has at least one scent."

422. Eldridge Cleaver, former leader of the Black Panthers, was born in Wabbeseka in 1935.

AMAZING ARKANSAS

423. Travis "Stonewall" Jackson, the baseball Hall of Famer who played shortstop for the N.Y. Giants, was born in Waldo on November 2, 1903.

424. Atkins is the pickle capital of Arkansas and hosts a Picklefest which includes pickle-eating and pickle juice-drinking contests. Sounds like a good dill to me.

425. At the age of 16, Bill Clinton went to Washington, D.C., through the American Legion Boy's Nation program and shook hands and had his picture taken with President John F. Kennedy.

426. Movie star, director and singer Dick Powell was born in Mountain View on November 14, 1904. He was also the host of TV's *Zane Grey Theater*.

427. Don't croak now, but Frog Fantasies in Eureka Springs features a sea of green frogs of all shapes and sizes from a collection more than 50 years old. Ribbet.

AMAZING ARKANSAS

428. Blind vocalist Al Hibler, who performed with Duke Ellington's orchestra in the 1940s, was born in Little Rock on August 16, 1915. He had a Top 10 pop hit in 1955 with *Unchained Melody*.

429. Baseball Hall of Fame's George Kell was born in Swifton on August 23, 1922. He won the American League batting title in 1949. Kell is now commissioner of the Arkansas Highway Department.

430. In 1936, King Bradford, "King of the Hitchhikers," thumbed his way across the state. He had already been to more than 4,000 towns and covered more than 45,000 miles before he hit Arkansas.

431. Kemmons Wilson, the founder of Holiday Inn, was born in Osceola on January 5, 1913. The original Holiday Inn opened in 1952 in Memphis.

AMAZING ARKANSAS

432. Booneville is the site each April of the "Cow Pasture Pool Tournament" when Newton Davis drives all his cattle out of the fields so that golfers can play a 12-hole tournament. 1955 U.S. Open champ Jack Fleck helped design the layout.

433. The "Merci" boxcar in Helena was a gift from France, who, after World War II, sent a "thank you train" of 48 cars to the United States. As the train toured the country, it dropped off one car at each state in gratitude for the war effort. Helena's boxcar is one of only five boxcars left.

434. Hamburg is the host each spring of an Armadillo Festival where armadillos race and tots vie for the title of Little Mr. and Mrs. Armadillo.

435. Hot Springs National Park is the only national park located in a city.

AMAZING ARKANSAS

436. Englishman Henry Stanley of Stanley and Livingston fame ("Dr. Livingston, I presume") lived and worked as a clerk in Varner, Arkansas, before his famous expedition into the African Congo.

437. Five to six thousands pounds of crawfish are consumed in two days each year at Dermott's annual Crawfish Festival.

438. Devil's Den State Park hosts an annual Bat-O-Rama with guided cave tours to see bats. It could drive you batty.

439. Springdale is home of the annual Albert E. Brumley Sundown to Sunup Gospel Sing, a celebration of gospel music.

440. The Arkansas State Dance is the square dance.

AMAZING ARKANSAS

441. Toad Suck near Conway was an Arkansas River ferry until 1970. Once the site of a tavern where rivermen enjoyed their liquor, it caused a traveler to comment, "Those fellows suck at a bottle 'til they swell up like toads." Now 'tis the site of the annual Toad Suck Daze. Hey, save me one of those T-shirts.

442. The first bridge built across the Arkansas River at Little Rock was a pontoon bridge constructed by Federal forces attacking the city in 1863. The Broadway Bridge between Little Rock and North Little Rock was completed on March 14, 1923.

443. The Old Almer Store in Helena used to be a riverboat, while Danville is the only town in Arkansas to be named after a riverboat.

444. Fayetteville was rated America's seventh best place to live by *Money* magazine in 1991.

AMAZING ARKANSAS

445. Bill Clinton's favorite McDonald's in Little Rock is located at 701 South Broadway. He often used the jog-through window. The first McDonald's in Arkansas was built in 1961 in Little Rock on University Avenue.

446. Quigley's Castle near Eureka Springs is one of the Ozarks' most peculiar houses with its suspended rooms and tropical plants which grow two-stories high.

447. The Hammond Museum of Bells in Eureka Springs has more than 1,000 bells on display. Ring-a-ding-ding.

448. Cotter, Arkansas, is called the "Trout Capital of the World," and *Southern Outdoors* magazine rates the White River as "America's best trout river."

AMAZING ARKANSAS

449. In 1937, farmer George Osborne of Siloam Springs grew "the world's tallest stalk of corn" at 19 feet and two inches high. For his efforts he won $150 and a tractor plow.

450. The Miracle Mansion in Eureka Springs has a Wonderful World of Miniatures which features all of the presidents and first ladies of the United States in miniature – except for the Bushes and the Clintons.

451. Be sure and tote an empty crock jar to Heber Springs' 10-acre Spring Park which features seven medicinal springs containing the mineral elements of black sulphur, red sulphur, white sulphur, iron, arsenic, magnesium and alum.

452. Poinsett County, Arkansas, was named after Joel R. Poinsett, who discovered the poinsettia plant in Mexico in 1828.

AMAZING ARKANSAS

453. Before its closing several years ago, the Mid-America Rosary Museum in North Little Rock had more than 1,500 rosaries on display and also collected surplus rosaries which were sent around the globe.

454. Manila boasts the Herman Davis Monument, whom Gen. John J. Pershing called "America's greatest hero" after Private Davis single-handedly saved an entire company during World War I.

455. Dale Evans, the Queen of the West and wife of Roy Rogers, grew up in Osceola where her grandfather was a doctor. She wrote Roy's theme song, *Happy Trails to You.*

456. John J. Audubon painted the willow flycatcher at Arkansas Post after it was first discovered there in 1822.

AMAZING ARKANSAS

457. Redfield, near Pine Bluff, features a drive-in restaurant, the Mammoth Orange, which is shaped like a giant orange. It came to fruition in 1956. On Friday nights, come watch the local boys peel out.

458. Attention! Arkansas supplied 29 generals for the Civil War, and while Helena's population was only 1,500, the town furnished seven generals to the Confederate army.

459. A world-record 68-pound 8-ounce smallmouth buffalo catfish was caught at Lake Hamilton on May 16, 1984, by Jerry Dolezal.

460. The Senior Walk at the University of Arkansas campus in Fayetteville is sidewalks containing the names of all the school's graduates beginning with the class of 1876.

AMAZING ARKANSAS

461. J.B. Hunt Transport Inc. was started in 1969 in Bentonville, Arkansas. Now headquartered in Lowell, Arkansas, it is the largest publicly held trucking company in the United States with its 6,900 trucks and 17,000 trailers.

462. The country's first direct dial long distance telephone call was made from Fordyce in 1960 from the Allied Telephone Company.

463. Arkansan Sam Walton received the nation's highest civilian award, the Presidential Medal of Freedom, on March 17, 1992, from President George Bush. The world's wealthiest man of 1985 said, "It was the greatest day of my life."

464. Hillary Clinton is the first First Lady with a post-graduate degree.

AMAZING ARKANSAS

465. Two million acres of land in the Territory of Arkansas were set aside by the federal government to satisfy land bounties promised to soldiers of the War of 1812. Most of the land was given to soldiers from Illinois and Indiana.

466. It's free. The Hot Springs produce over one million gallons of hot water daily, and in downtown Hot Springs there are faucets where you can get all you want for free. Bring up your jug and fill up your mug with that good ole mountain dew.

467. Harrison calls itself "the crossroads of the Ozarks" and each May hosts the Crooked Creek Crawdad Festival.

468. The first time chloroform was used by a dentist in Arkansas was on August 31, 1849.

AMAZING ARKANSAS

469. The Arkansas bear-hunting season is from November 1-15 with a limit of one. No dogs allowed.

470. The International Mule Jump Festival is held in the Pea Ridge City Park, where mules have cleared barriers over six feet high. Jumping Jacks!

471. Senator J. William Fulbright served for several years as chairman of the Senate Foreign Relations Committee, and is still considered an expert in non-domestic policy. Congressman Wilbur Mills of Kensett served for several years as chairman of the House Ways and Means Committee, making him one of the most powerful men on Capitol Hill.

472. Singer and western film star Jimmy Wakely (*Slipping Around*) was born near Mineola on February 16, 1914.

AMAZING ARKANSAS

473. Five flags have been raised over Arkansas soil: France, Spain, the U.S., the Confederacy and the Arkansas state flag.

474. Piggott native Frances Greer was a Metropolitan opera star who retired in 1954 to become a professor at the University of Michigan School of Music. As a baby, she hummed *Over There* while nursing, according to her mother.

475. The world premiere of *True Grit* was held in Little Rock on June 12, 1969, as a fund-raiser for the Democrat party. Tickets to the affair at the Cinema 150 were $50. Glen Campbell, who starred in the film, was present at the event. The second premiere was held in Hot Springs the next day at which Charles Portis, the book's author attended. Portis didn't agree with the first showing being used to raise money for politics.

AMAZING ARKANSAS

476. The Arkansas Democrat-Gazette is delivered daily by jet to the White House where it arrives by 11:15 a.m.

477. Paris, Arkansas, had 63 coal mines in 1937.

478. Arkansas is the only state surrounded by states, in which you can reach all the bordering states by traveling south.

479. Arkansas had a literal giant. Jim Tarver of Turrell was 8-feet 6-inches tall and weighed 450 pounds in 1937.

480. The Arkansas state auditor in 1938, Oscar Humphreys, was an expert penman and marksman and drove a car, yet he had no arms.

481. Joe T. Robinson was an Arkansas congressman, governor and senator, all in one year, 1913.

AMAZING ARKANSAS

482. Wynne was home of the world's largest red raspberry farm at one time.

483. In 1941, the Arkansas Ordinance Plant opened in Jacksonville to manufacture arms for the war and Jacksonville became a boomtown. At its peak during World War II, 42,000 people lived and worked there. Nine trains a day shuttled workers to and from Little Rock, while inner-city buses ran every thirty minutes. At Sunnyside Housing, as many as twenty homes were built in twenty-four hours.

484. Magnet Cove has more than 65 valuable minerals in its earth, more than any other spot in the world of comparable size. That's a lode of stone.

485. Pink, gray, red, black, white, chocolate and green marble have been quarried in north Arkansas. Makes you hungry doesn't it?

AMAZING ARKANSAS

486. Four Arkansas governors came from one German colony in Virginia (James Conway, H.M. Rector, Elias Conway and W.M. Fishback). William R. Miller of Batesville was the first native-born governor of Arkansas. When he was elected in 1878, he received 100 percent of the votes cast.

487. In the early 1900s, the Hope Gazette published the New Testament as a serial.

488. The oldest college in Arkansas is the University of the Ozarks in Clarksville, founded by the Cumberland Presbyterians in 1834.

489. Baseball Hall of Fame member and New York Yankee catcher Bill Dickey grew up in Kensett. He had a career batting average of .313. Bill's brother George "Skeets" Dickey also played major league baseball.

AMAZING ARKANSAS

490. Arkansas is the only state in which the theory of evolution was outlawed by a vote of the people. In a 1927 election, the consensus was 108,991 against the theory and 63,406 for it.

491. Robert H. Crockett, a DeWitt lawyer and editor and grandson of Davy Crockett, always wore a Prince Albert coat and kid gloves, even when the temperature was over 100 degrees in the shade.

492. Willie Shoemaker was the first jockey to win 100 stakes races worth $100,000 or more. He won his 100th stakes race at Oaklawn in Hot Springs on March 30th, 1974. If the shoe fits, ride it.

493. Albert Pike, associate justice of the Arkansas supreme court and lawyer, soldier, poet and statesman, was recognized by the Masonic fraternity as the highest authority in the world on Masonic law and symbolism.

AMAZING ARKANSAS

494. Little Rock leads the nation in Ro-Tel Tomatoes and Green Chilis consumption, using more than twice as much as the second largest market. One million and eight hundred thousand cans were sold in Little Rock in 1992. Another glass of water, please.

495. Helena was described by Mark Twain in *Life on the Mississippi* as "one of the prettiest situations on the river." One of the highlights of Roger Miller's Tony Award-winning musical *Big River,* based on Mark Twain's *Huckleberry Finn,* is the tune *Arkansas/How Blest We Are.*

496. Ice skates were sold for the first time in Little Rock in 1880 when the Arkansas River froze over. But Hot Springs beat them to the punch when it came to indoor recreation since it had the state's first bowling alley in 1853.

AMAZING ARKANSAS

497. Some historians believe a cannonball fired June 17, 1862, from the Federal ironclad Mound City on the White River at St. Charles was the single most destructive shot of the Civil War. The projectile struck a steam pipe and killed nearly 100 soldiers.

498. On November 13, 1833, in the night skies over Arkansas "a great display of falling stars was seen from 4 a.m. until daybreak."

499. Among the stars of the Orton Circus, which came through the state in 1867, were Billy Andrews, billed as "the funniest man alive," and Andy Gaffney, the Human Cannonball. If Andrews was the first one to perform on the bill, we guess it is possible that Gaffney died laughing.

500. For tourist information about Arkansas, call 1-800-NATURAL.

ARKANSAS POSTSCRIPT

We've done our darndest to include the most amazing Arkansas facts we could find. If you have another amazing fact about Arkansas that you think should have been mentioned in this book, then please drop a line to our attention, in care of Floyd's Barbershop, 8617 Barber Street, North Little Rock, Arkansas 72120.

We'll appreciate it.

SELECTED REFERENCES

Arkansans of the Years, Fay Williams, C.C. Allard and Associates, 1951, 1952, 1953, 1954

Arkansas, C. Fred Williams, Windsor Publications, 1986

Arkansas: A Guide to the State, Federal Writers Program, Hastings House, 1941

Arkansas: Off the Beaten Path, Patti DeLano, The Globe Pequot Press, 1992

Arkansas Almanac, Lawrence Harper, editor, Arkansas Almanac Inc.

Arkansas Calendar of Events, state of Arkansas, 1993

The Arkansas Challenge, Avantus Green, 1966

The Arkansas Democrat, various issues

The Arkansas Democrat-Gazette, various issues

The Arkansas Gazette, various issues

The Arkansas Handbook, 1937-1950, Dallas T. Herndon, Arkansas Historical Commission

The Arkansas Handbook, Diane Smith, Emerald City Press, 1984

Arkansas Roadsides, Bill Earngey, East Mountain Press, 1987
Arkansas Times, June 1986
Arkansas Tour Guide, state of Arkansas, 1993
Arkansas Video Almanac, Jones Productions Inc. 1992
The Atlas of Arkansas, Richard Smith, University of Arkansas Press, 1989
The Billboard Book of Top 40 Hits, Joel Whitburn, Billboard Publications, 1983
The Complete All-Time Pro Baseball Register, David S. Neft, Richard M. Cohen and Jordan A. Deutsch, Tempo Books, 1979
The Country Music Foundation, Nashville, Tenn.
The Encyclopedia of Folk, Country & Western Music, Irwin Stambler and Grelun Landon, St. Martin's Press, 1983
Eureka Springs, Eureka Springs Chamber of Commerce, 1992

Gravely the Mules Stopped Dancing, Charles Allbright, August House, 1988
Greater Little Rock, Jim Lester and Judy Lester, The Donning Company, 1986
Greater Little Rock, Windor Press, 1990
Guinness Book of World Records, Bantam Books, 1992
High lights of Arkansas History, Dallas T. Herndon, Arkansas Historical Commission, 1922
Hillary Clinton, The Inside Story, Judith Warner, Signet, 1993
A History - North Little Rock, The Unique City, Walter Adams, August House, 1986
Joel Whitburn's Top Country Singles, 1944-1988, Record Research Inc.
The Jungles of Arkansas, A Personal History of the Wonder State, Bob Lancaster, The University of Arkansas Press, 1989
Million Selling Records from the 1900s to the 1980s, Joseph Murrells, Arco Publishing, 1984
The New York Times Book of Sports Legends, Joseph J. Vecchione, Times Books, 1991

Parade Magazine, April 11, 1993
The Roads of Arkansas, Shearer Publishing, 1990
Searcy, Arkansas: A Frontier Town Grows Up With America, Raymond Lee Muncy, Harding Press, 1976
"Tell Me About Arkansas," Tucker Steinmetz, Department of Arkansas History, 1988
This Is Arkansas, the Arkansas Association of County Judges, Inc. 1976
Thunderstorms, Derek W.G. Sears, University of Arkansas Press, 1988
The TV Encyclopedia, David Inman, Perigee Books, 1991
TV Movies and Video Guide, Leonard Maltin, Signet, 1993
USA Weekend, Jan. 15, Jan. 22, July 4, 1993
Welcome to Blanchard Springs Caverns Arkansas, United States Department of Agriculture, 1991
Who's Who in Entertainment, 1992-93, Reed Publishing, 1992
With This We Challenge ... An Epitome of Arkansas, Avantus Green, 1945

How To Order This Book

If your local bookstore is out of *Amazing Arkansas,* and you'd like to have a couple of extra copies to mail to your aunt in Tennessee and that cousin who moved to California in 1972, you can order extra copies directly from us by sending check or money order for $5.95 per book plus $1.00 each for shipping and handling. Mail to Spring Creek Books, P.O. Box 159015, Nashville, TN 37215. Allow 4-6 weeks for delivery.